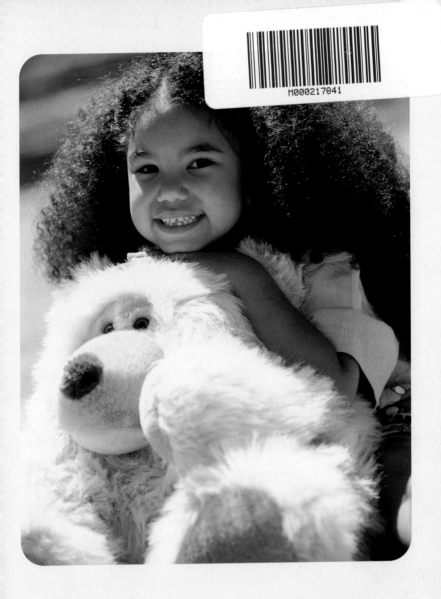

Today is my birthday.
I will have a party.

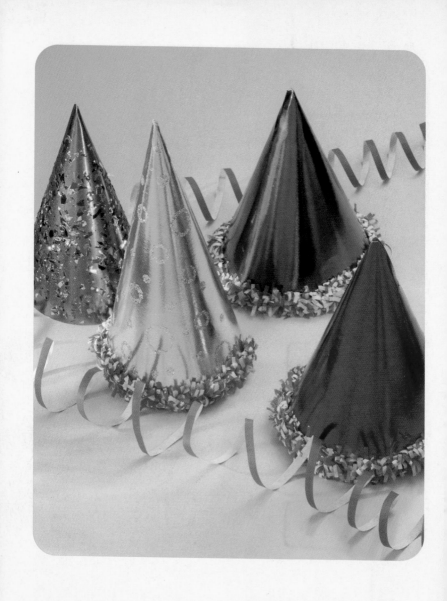

I will have party hats.

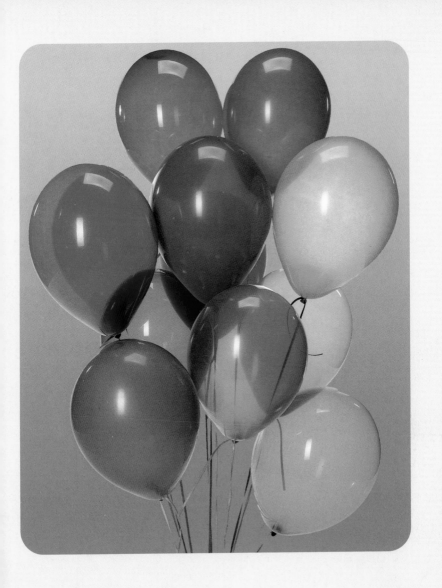

I will have balloons.

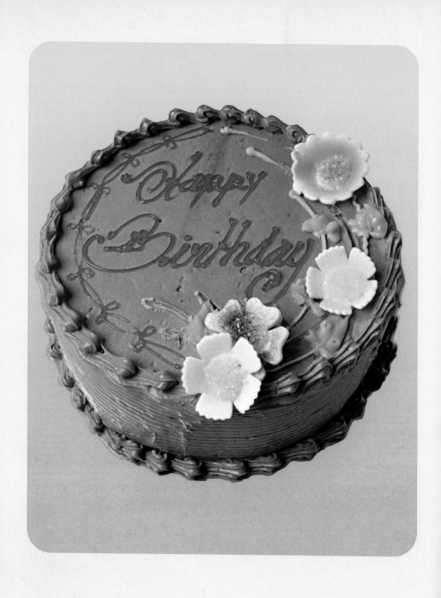

I will have a cake.

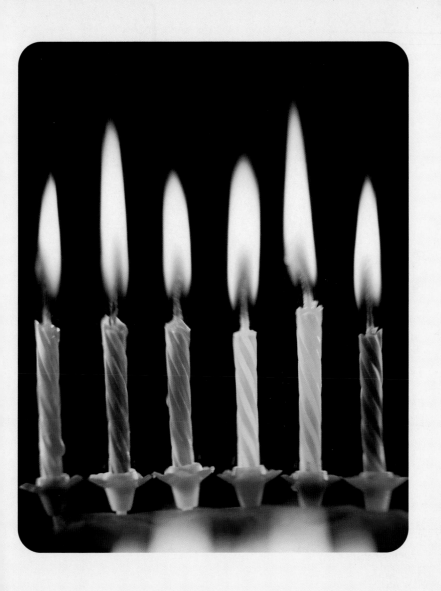

I will have candles.

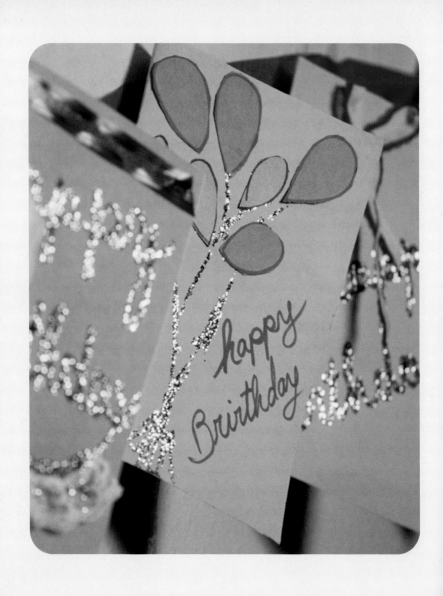

I will get cards.

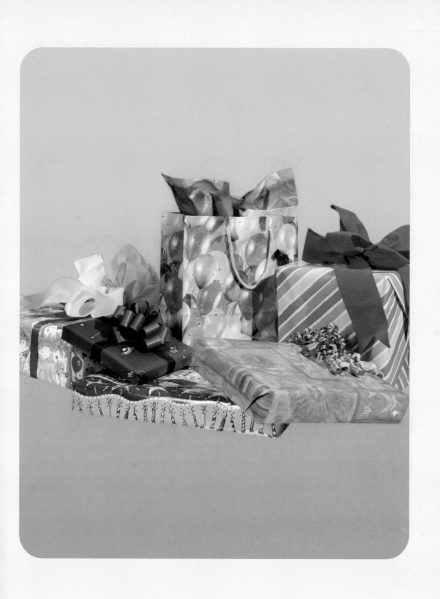

I will get presents.

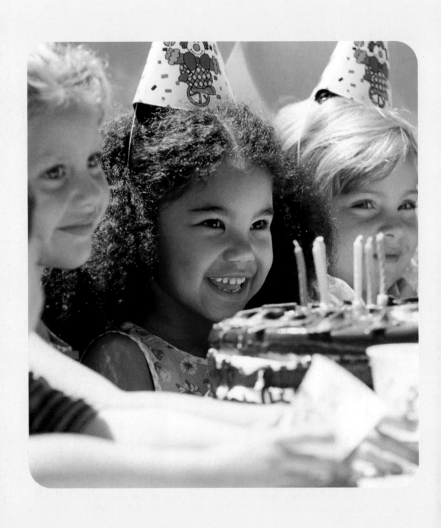

My friends and I will have fun!